I HAVE

Collected Poems of
Love, Loss, & Emotion

BY

Dylan Thomas

Published by Ragged Hand,

an imprint of Read & Co.

This edition published by Read & Co. in 2024

Extra material © 2024 Read & Co. Books

All rights reserved. No portion of this book may be reproduced in any form without the permission of the publisher in writing.

A catalogue record for this book is available from the British Library.

ISBN: 9781528723398

Front Cover: *Hill with Two Figures: View from the Artist's Studio*
Painted by Gwen John (1876-1939)

Read & Co. is part of Read Books Ltd.
For more information visit www.readandcobooks.co.uk

Contents

Dylan Thomas - The Life and Works of the Welsh Poet.........5

Especially when the October Wind 19

The Hunchback in the Park...................................21

I Have Longed to Move Away 24

Find Meat on Bones..25

The Tombstone Told When She Died......................28

In the Beginning 30

From Love's First Fever to Her Plague......................32

When Once the Twilight Locks No Longer 35

Should Lanterns Shine 38

Where Once the Waters of Your Face 39

If I Were Tickled by the Rub of Love 41

Altarwise by Owl-Light 44

A Grief Ago..54

I Make this in a Warring Absence 57

When All My Five and Country Senses See 61

Paper and Sticks...62

On a Wedding Anniversary..................................63

Love in the Asylum 64

The Ballad of the Long-Legged Bait........................66

Into Her Lying Down Head 77

Lie Still, Sleep Becalmed 83

In My Craft or Sullen Art..................................84

The Conversation of Prayers 85

In the White Giant's Thigh 87

Lament...91

Bibliography..95

Dylan Thomas
The Life and Works of the Welsh Poet

Reaching celebrity acclaim during his lifetime, Dylan Thomas is one of the most recognisable poets of the twentieth century. Familiar to many as an erratic yet ingenious writer, he's known for his intensely emotional and beautifully lyrical works, such as the poems 'Fern Hill' (1945) and 'Do Not Go Gentle Into That Good Night' (1951), as well as the influential radio drama *Under Milk Wood* (1954). Born and raised in Swansea on the south-west coast of Wales, he was often described as a soft, quiet, sickly child, but later became a British media star and is now considered one of the greatest literary voices in Welsh history.

Born on the 27th of October 1914, Dylan Thomas was the second child of Florence Hannah (1882–1958) and David John Thomas (1876–1952). Along with his elder sister, Nancy (1906–1953), Thomas was raised bilingual, speaking both Welsh and English, surrounded by family at their Cwmdonkin Drive home in Swansea. Thomas first began education by attending a private school close to his family home before enrolling at Swansea Grammar School for Boys in 1925, where his father taught English. He wasn't known to be a particularly bright or participatory pupil, preferring to engage in drama groups and reading rather than traditional schooling. His interest in poetry developed early in his childhood, and during his first year he submitted a poem to the school's magazine, and his work was printed in the publication. He eventually went on to become the magazine's editor.

Leaving school at 16, Thomas began working for the *South Wales Daily Post* as a reporter. Still living with his parents, he left his job in 1931 and began working as a freelance journalist while also concentrating on his poetry. He continued this method of working for several years, and during this time, he amassed over 200 poems in the notebooks he started keeping as a schoolboy. Between 1930 and 1934, much of his poetry was published, including 'Before I Knocked', 'The Force That Through the Green Fuse Drives the Flower', and 'And Death Shall Have No Dominion', the last of which was printed in the *New English Weekly* in 1933.

In 1934, the poet's literary career really took off. Thomas moved to London, where *The Listener*—a magazine established by the BBC in 1929—published his 'Light Breaks Where No Sun Shines'. The seminal poem garnered attention from three of London's most revered literary minds: T. S. Eliot, Geoffrey Grigson, and Stephen Spender, who went on to assist him in publishing his first collection of poetry, *18 Poems* (1934). The volume laid the foundations for much of his work, introducing him and his unique style as a modernist poet. His rhyming verse was largely influenced by the Romantics and followed strict rules of metre and syntax while demonstrating rich emotional intensity. This was a distinctive style at the time of publication, contrasting Thomas' contemporaries such as W. H. Auden, who is often described as an anti-Romantic poet. *18 Poems* has a heavy focus on death, loss, and love, which are themes often employed in Thomas' work, and his candid exploration of dark subjects helped to establish his name in literature.

Thomas met Caitlin Macnamara (1913–1994) in the early months of 1936. The 22-year-old had run away from home to make her name as a dancer and was working as a chorus girl at the London Palladium when she met the poet in a West End pub, The Wheatsheaf. Despite the fact Caitlin was seeing the Welsh artist Augustus John at the time, Thomas drunkenly lay down in her lap and proposed. Both Thomas and Caitlin later stated that they promptly left the pub together and had been in correspondence since. They were married on the 11th of July 1937 in Penzance, Cornwall. The couple moved back to Wales together in 1938, and it was here that Llewelyn Edouard, their first child, was born on the 30th of January 1939.

During the first year of their courtship in 1936, renowned British publisher J. M. Dent released Thomas' second collection of poetry, *Twenty-five Poems*. The book was critically acclaimed upon publication, and it was just two years later that Thomas was awarded the Oscar Blumenthal Prize for Poetry and offered a contract with New Directions, a publishing house based in New

York City. His following volumes, however, were less successful. *The Map of Love* (1939) was a collection of 16 poems and seven short fantasy stories, while *Portrait of the Artist as a Young Dog* (1940) collated ten fictionalised memoirs. As the success of his work dwindled, Thomas was forced to rely on the generosity of his friends and family for financial support. Margaret Taylor was one of his most loyal patrons, finding and purchasing properties in Oxford and Wales for the family to reside. It was Taylor who bought Thomas his famed, final home: the Boathouse.

When the Second World War broke out in September 1939, Thomas considered registering as a conscientious objector due to his pacifistic and anti-war beliefs. He was unable to be drafted, however, after being categorised as a C3 (poor physical specimen) by military recruitment due to his asthma sometimes confining him to bed.

In May of 1941, Thomas and Caitlin left their first child with his grandmother and moved back to London. The poet found work with the Ministry of Information, working as a scriptwriter for a documentary series about patriotism and urban planning in wartime. He also began receiving intermittent income from the BBC, and in 1943, Thomas recorded 'Reminiscences of Childhood', a 15-minute talk, for the Welsh BBC.

Throughout his marriage, Thomas had numerous affairs. One of which began in early 1943 when he met Pamela Glendower, a journalistic editor. While the secret relationship bloomed, Caitlin was pregnant with Thomas' second child. Aeronwy was born in March of that year, and the affair eventually petered out after the war's end.

In September 1944, the family moved to New Quay and rented a cliff-top bungalow overlooking Cardigan Bay. While in this secluded home, Thomas wrote his masterful poem 'Fern Hill', reflecting on his happily naive childhood, and began work on his radio play *Under Milk Wood*, then titled *Quite Early One Morning*. In December of that year, he recorded a reading of the play for the Welsh BBC, and it was later broadcast by the BBC Home Service on 31st August 1945. Between then and 1949, he recorded over 100 broadcasts for the corporation.

The poetry collection that made Thomas his reputation was *Deaths and Entrances,* published in 1946. The volume features works influenced by the war and includes 'Fern Hill' as well as other celebrated poems by Thomas, such as 'In My Craft or Sullen Art' and 'Poem in October'. The book's success saw the poet travel across the UK and Europe on a Society of Authors scholarship.

In May of 1949, the family moved to the Boathouse at Laugharne. This property was home to Thomas' famous writing shed, situated on a cliff's edge just a hundred yards from the main house, where he wrote some of his most beloved and critically acclaimed work. His third child, Colm Garan Hart, was born just a few months later.

In February 1950, Thomas embarked on his first journey to the United States of America after being invited to tour his work by the American poet John Brinnin. He would visit the country just four times before his death on the final trip in 1953. His first tour commenced at the Kaufmann Auditorium of the New York Poetry Centre and took place over three months across 40 venues.

As 1950 drew to a close, and with his father battling throat cancer, Thomas wrote one of his most beloved poems, 'Do Not Go Gentle Into That Good Night'. Focusing on the acceptance of death, the lyrical examination of loss is a hauntingly beautiful work that has resonated with many in the decades since its publication. Often chosen for funeral readings, the poem is addressed to his father and gently encourages readers to value the beauty in life.

Becoming one of the first poets to have his work recorded on vinyl, Thomas' poetry was released with Caedmon Records in late 1952. That same year, a shortened early draft of *Under Milk Wood* was published in the *Botteghe Oscure* literary journal under the title of 'Llareggub'—a fictional name devised from reversing the term 'bugger all'—but the title was later changed to help attract American audiences. J. M. Dent published Thomas' final collection of poems, *Collected Poems*, on the 10th of November 1952, and the volume went on to win the Foyle Poetry Prize.

Thomas' second tour of the US also began that year, with Caitlin accompanying him. Having become known for his excessive drinking habits and rude, outlandish personality, Thomas drank in unhealthily large quantities to keep up this appearance and entertain his fans and contemporaries. Over a lengthy tour of 46 venues, the poet began to experience lung and gout troubles, furthering his health problems.

His father passed away just before Christmas in 1952, and tragedy and grief continued to haunt Thomas in the following months. In early 1953, Caitlin had an abortion, his older sister, Nancy, died from liver cancer, one of his patrons overdosed, and three of his close friends passed away at a young age.

He returned to the US alone in April 1953 for a third tour and saw *Under Milk Wood* performed by a full cast for the first time in May. During this tour, he spent a large amount of time with John Brinnin's assistant, Liz Reitell, with whom he had an affair. He began receiving treatment from Reitell's family physician, Milton Feltenstein, after falling down the stairs and fracturing his arm. On his return to the United Kingdom, Thomas's health was dwindling, with him reportedly suffering blackouts and considerable coughing attacks, now relying on an inhaler.

There has been lots of controversy and conflicting information surrounding Thomas' final days and the cause of his death. His last trip to New York commenced in October 1953, and he spent his days rehearsing for the stage production of *Under Milk Wood*.

As he worked tirelessly during the day and drank to excess most evenings, he increasingly struggled with his asthma. The smog in the city had risen to dangerous levels for those who suffered chest and lung-related illnesses, and by the end of November, over 200 New York City citizens had died due to the air pollution. Thomas was progressively declining in health, over working and over drinking. On the 4th of November, he spent the day confined to his hotel room by sickness. The poet was visited by Feltenstein three times and administered with injections of painkillers. During his last visit, the doctor injected Thomas with half a grain of morphine, sending him into a coma from which he never recovered. He passed away in St Vincent's Hospital on the 9th of November 1953, aged 39. He was buried in the Laugharne churchyard in Wales, where Caitlin was also laid to rest when she died in 1994.

A year after the death of Dylan Thomas, the BBC broadcasted the full, final version of his masterful radio play, *Under Milk Wood*. The first broadcast starred Richard Burton, and the actor was joined in the later film adaptation by Elizabeth Taylor in 1972. Globally celebrated, he is remembered as one of the most important modernist poets of Wales and Britain.

He died a celebrity, and in the decades following, as his work has been translated and adapted around the world, his fame has grown. Thomas' writing confronted the questions others shied away from, exploring the poignancy of death, grief, and love with unwavering courage and beauty. His masterful lyricism and vivid imagery transported poetic ideals of small-town life in Wales into universal experience.

Lizzie Stoddart
Bristol, 2023

'Thomas has the bardic consciousness: he writes a personal lyric in which the sense of his own history and name is surrounded by strange lights and glooms, and if his poems are often obscure, it is that they obey nocturnal laws. His poetry exists in a world in which the sexual forces of nature, the shifting tides and currents for which the individual cannot fully account but to which the passion of his being is finally responsible, override the merely personal clamor.'

—*The Nation*, 2nd May 1953

I HAVE LONGED

Especially when the October Wind

Especially when the October wind
With frosty fingers punishes my hair,
Caught by the crabbing sun I walk on fire
And cast a shadow crab upon the land,
By the sea's side, hearing the noise of birds,
Hearing the raven cough in winter sticks,
My busy heart who shudders as she talks
Sheds the syllabic blood and drains her words.

Shut, too, in a tower of words, I mark
On the horizon walking like the trees
The wordy shapes of women, and the rows
Of the star-gestured children in the park.
Some let me make you of the vowelled beeches,
Some of the oaken voices, from the roots
Of many a thorny shire tell you notes,
Some let me make you of the water's speeches.

Behind a pot of ferns the wagging clock
Tells me the hour's word, the neural meaning
Flies on the shafted disk, declaims the morning
And tells the windy weather in the cock.
Some let me make you of the meadow's signs;
The signal grass that tells me all I know
Breaks with the wormy winter through the eye.
Some let me tell you of the raven's sins.

Especially when the October wind
(Some let me make you of autumnal spells,
The spider-tongued, and the loud hill of Wales)
With fists of turnips punishes the land,
Some let me make you of the heartless words.
The heart is drained that, spelling in the scurry
Of chemic blood, warned of the coming fury.
By the sea's side hear the dark-vowelled birds.

The Hunchback in the Park

The hunchback in the park
A solitary mister
Propped between trees and water
From the opening of the garden lock
That lets the trees and water enter
Until the Sunday sombre bell at dark

Eating bread from a newspaper
Drinking water from the chained cup
That the children filled with gravel
In the fountain basin where I sailed my ship
Slept at night in a dog kennel
But nobody chained him up.

Like the park birds he came early
Like the water he sat down
And Mister they called Hey mister
The truant boys from the town
Running when he had heard them clearly
On out of sound

Past lake and rockery
Laughing when he shook his paper
Hunchbacked in mockery
Through the loud zoo of the willow groves
Dodging the park keeper
With his stick that picked up leaves.

And the old dog sleeper
Alone between nurses and swans
While the boys among willows
Made the tigers jump out of their eyes
To roar on the rockery stones
And the groves were blue with sailors

Made all day until bell time
A woman figure without fault
Straight as a young elm
Straight and tall from his crooked bones
That she might stand in the night
After the locks and chains

All night in the unmade park
After the railings and shrubberies
The birds the grass the trees the lake
And the wild boys innocent as strawberries
Had followed the hunchback
To his kennel in the dark.

I Have Longed to Move Away

I have longed to move away
From the hissing of the spent lie
And the old terrors' continual cry
Growing more terrible as the day
Goes over the hill into the deep sea;
I have longed to move away
From the repetition of salutes,
For there are ghosts in the air
And ghostly echoes on paper,
And the thunder of calls and notes.

I have longed to move away but am afraid;
Some life, yet unspent, might explode
Out of the old lie burning on the ground,
And, crackling into the air, leave me half-blind.
Neither by night's ancient fear,
The parting of hat from hair,
Pursed lips at the receiver,
Shall I fall to death's feather.
By these I would not care to die,
Half convention and half lie.

Find Meat on Bones

'Find meat on bones that soon have none,
And drink in the two milked crags,
The merriest marrow and the dregs
Before the ladies' breasts are hags
And the limbs are torn.
Disturb no winding-sheets, my son,
But when the ladies are cold as stone
Then hang a ram rose over the rags.

'Rebel against the binding moon
And the parliament of sky,
The kingcrafts of the wicked sea,
Autocracy of night and day,
Dictatorship of sun.
Rebel against the flesh and bone,
The word of the blood, the wily skin,
And the maggot no man can slay.'

'The thirst is quenched, the hunger gone,
And my heart is cracked across;
My face is haggard in the glass,
My lips are withered with a kiss,
My breasts are thin.
A merry girl took me for man,
I laid her down and told her sin,
And put beside her a ram rose.

'The maggot that no man can kill
And the man no rope can hang
Rebel against my father's dream
That out of a bower of red swine
Howls the foul fiend to heel.
I cannot murder, like a fool,
Season and sunshine, grace and girl,
Nor can I smother the sweet waking.'

Black night still ministers the moon,
And the sky lays down her laws,
The sea speaks in a kingly voice,
Light and dark are no enemies
But one companion.
'War on the spider and the wren!
War on the destiny of man!
Doom on the sun!'
Before death takes you, O take back this

The Tombstone Told When She Died

The tombstone told when she died.
Her two surnames stopped me still.
A virgin married at rest.
She married in this pouring place,
That I struck one day by luck,
Before I heard in my mother's side
Or saw in the looking-glass shell
The rain through her cold heart speak
And the sun killed in her face.
More the thick stone cannot tell.
Before she lay on a stranger's bed
With a hand plunged through her hair,
Or that rainy tongue beat back
Through the devilish years and innocent deaths
To the room of a secret child,
Among men later I heard it said
She cried her white-dressed limbs were bare
And her red lips were kissed black,
She wept in her pain and made mouths,
Talked and tore though her eyes smiled.

I who saw in a hurried film
Death and this mad heroine
Meet once on a mortal wall
Heard her speak through the chipped beak
Of the stone bird guarding her:
I died before bedtime came
But my womb was bellowing
And I felt with my bare fall
A blazing red harsh head tear up
And the dear floods of his hair.

In the Beginning

In the beginning was the three-pointed star,
One smile of light across the empty face,
One bough of bone across the rooting air,
The substance forked that marrowed the first sun,
And, burning ciphers on the round of space,
Heaven and hell mixed as they spun.

In the beginning was the pale signature,
Three-syllabled and starry as the smile,
And after came the imprints on the water,
Stamp of the minted face upon the moon;
The blood that touched the crosstree and the grail
Touched the first cloud and left a sign.

In the beginning was the mounting fire
That set alight the weathers from a spark,
A three-eyed, red-eyed spark, blunt as a flower,
Life rose and spouted from the rolling seas,
Burst in the roots, pumped from the earth and rock
The secret oils that drive the grass.

In the beginning was the word, the word
That from the solid bases of the light
Abstracted all the letters of the void;
And from the cloudy bases of the breath
The word flowed up, translating to the heart
First characters of birth and death.

In the beginning was the secret brain.
The brain was celled and soldered in the thought
Before the pitch was forking to a sun;
Before the veins were shaking in their sieve,
Blood shot and scattered to the winds of light
The ribbed original of love.

From Love's First Fever to Her Plague

From love's first fever to her plague, from the soft second
And the hollow minute of the womb,
From the unfolding to the scissored caul,
The time for breast and the green apron age
When no mouth stirred about the hanging famine,
All world was one, one windy nothing,
My world was christened in a stream of milk.
And earth and sky were as one airy light.

From the first print of the unshodden foot, the lifting
Hand, the breaking of the hair,
From the first secret of the heart, the warning ghost,
And to the first dumb wonder at the flesh,
Th sun was red, the moon was grey,
The earth and sky were as two mountains meeting.

The body prospered, teeth in the marrowed gums,
The growing bones, the rumour of manseed
Within the hallowed gland, blood blessed the heart,
And the four winds, that had long blown as one,
Shone in my ears the light of sound,
Called in my eyes the sound of light.
And yellow was the multiplying sand,
Each golden grain spat life into its fellow,
Green was the singing of the house.

The plum my mother picked matured slowly,
The boy she dropped from darkness at her side
Into the sided lap of light grew strong,
Was muscled, matted, wise to the crying thigh
And to the voice that, like a voice of hunger,
Itched in the noise of wind and sun.

And from the first declension of the flesh
I learnt man's tongue, to twist the shapes of thoughts
To shade and knit anew the patch of words
Left by the dead who, in their moonless acre,
Need no word's warmth.
The root of tongues ends in a spentout cancer,
That but a name, where maggots have their X.

I learnt the verbs of will, and had my secret;
The code of night tapped on my tongue;
What had been one was many sounding minded.

One womb, one mind, spewed out the matter,
One breast gave suck the fever's issue;
From the divorcing sky I learnt the double,
The two-framed globe that spun into a score;
A million minds gave suck to such a bud
As forks my eye;
Youth did condense; the tears of spring
Dissolved in summer and the hundred seasons;
One sun, one manna, warmed and fed.

When Once the Twilight Locks No Longer

When once the twilight locks no longer
Locked in the long worm of my finger
Nor damned the sea that sped about my fist,
The mouth of time sucked, like a sponge,
The milky acid on each hinge,
And swallowed dry the waters of the breast.

When galactic sea was sucked
And all the dry seabed unlocked,
I sent my creature scouting on the globe,
That globe itself of hair and bone
That, sewn to me by nerve and brain,
Had stringed my flask of matter to his rib.

My fuses timed to charge his heart,
He blew like powder to the light
And held a little sabbath with the sun,
But when the stars, assuming shape,
Drew in his eyes the straws of sleep,
He drowned his father's magics in a dream.

All issue armoured, of the grave,
The redhaired cancer still alive,
The cataracted eyes that filmed their cloth;
Some dead undid their bushy jaws,
And bags of blood let out their flies;
He had by heart the Christ-cross-row of death.

Sleep navigates the tides of time;
The dry Sargasso of the tomb
Gives up its dead to such a working sea;
And sleep rolls mute above the beds
Where fishes' food is fed the shades
Who periscope through flowers to the sky.

When once the twilight screws were turned,
And mother milk was stiff as sand,
I sent my own ambassador to light;
By trick or chance he fell asleep
And conjured up a carcass shape
To rob me of my fluids in his heart.

Awake, my sleeper, to the sun,
A worker in the morning town,
And leave the poppied pickthank where he lies;
The fences of the light are down,
All but the brisket riders thrown,
And worlds hang on the trees.

Should Lanterns Shine

Should lanterns shine, the holy face,
Caught in an octagon of unaccustomed light,
Would wither up, and any boy of love
Look twice before he fell from grace.
The features in their private dark
Are formed of flesh, but let the false day come
And from her lips the faded pigments fall,
The mummy cloths expose an ancient breast.

I have been told to reason by the heart,
But heart, like head, leads helplessly;
I have been told to reason by the pulse,
And, when it quickens, alter the actions' pace
Till field and roof lie level and the same
So fast I move defying time, the quiet gentleman
Whose beard wags in Egyptian wind.

I have heard many years of telling,
And many years should see some change.

The ball I threw while playing in the park
Has not yet reached the ground.

Where Once the Waters of Your Face

Where once the waters of your face
Spun to my screws, your dry ghost blows,
The dead turns up its eye;
Where once the mermen through your ice
Pushed up their hair, the dry wind steers
Through salt and root and roe.

Where once your green knots sank their splice
Into the tided cord, there goes
The green unraveller,
His scissors oiled, his knife hung loose
To cut the channels at their source
And lay the wet fruits low.

Invisible, your clocking tides
Break on the lovebeds of the weeds;
The weed of love's left dry;
There round about your stones the shades
Of children go who, from their voids,
Cry to the dolphined sea.

Dry as a tomb, your coloured lids
Shall not be latched while magic glides
Sage on the earth and sky;
There shall be corals in your beds,
There shall be serpents in your tides,
Till all our sea-faiths die.

If I Were Tickled by the Rub of Love

If I were tickled by the rub of love,
A rooking girl who stole me for her side,
Broke through her straws, breaking my bandaged string,
If the red tickle as the cattle calve
Still set to scratch a laughter from my lung,
I would not fear the apple nor the flood
Nor the bad blood of spring.

Shall it be male or female? say the cells,
And drop the plum like fire from the flesh.
If I were tickled by the hatching hair,
The winging bone that sprouted in the heels,
The itch of man upon the baby's thigh,
I would not fear the gallows nor the axe
Nor the crossed sticks of war.

Shall it be male or female? say the fingers
That chalk the walls with green girls and their men.
I would not fear the muscling-in of love
If I were tickled by the urchin hungers
Rehearsing heat upon a raw-edged nerve.
I would not fear the devil in the loin
Nor the outspoken grave.

If I were tickled by the lovers' rub
That wipes away not crow's-foot nor the lock
Of sick old manhood on the fallen jaws,
Time and the crabs and the sweethearting crib
Would leave me cold as butter for the flies,
The sea of scums could drown me as it broke
Dead on the sweethearts' toes.

This world is half the devil's and my own,
Daft with the drug that's smoking in a girl
And curling round the bud that forks her eye.
An old man's shank one-marrowed with my bone,
And all the herrings smelling in the sea,
I sit and watch the worm beneath my nail
Wearing the quick away.

And that's the rub, the only rub that tickles.
The knobbly ape that swings along his sex
From damp love-darkness and the nurse's twist
Can never raise the midnight of a chuckle,
Nor when he finds a beauty in the breast
Of lover, mother, lovers, or his six
Feet in the rubbing dust.

And what's the rub? Death's feather on the nerve?
Your mouth, my love, the thistle in the kiss?
My Jack of Christ born thorny on the tree?
The words of death are dryer than his stiff,
My wordy wounds are printed with your hair.
I would be tickled by the rub that is:
Man be my metaphor.

Altarwise by Owl-Light

I

Altarwise by owl-light in the half-way house
The gentleman lay graveward with his furies;
Abaddon in the hangnail cracked from Adam,
And, from his fork, a dog among the fairies,
The atlas-eater with a jaw for news,
Bit out the mandrake with to-morrows scream.
Then, penny-eyed, that gentlemen of wounds,
Old cock from nowheres and the heaven's egg,
With bones unbuttoned to the half-way winds,
Hatched from the windy salvage on one leg,
Scraped at my cradle in a walking word
That night of time under the Christward shelter:
I am the long world's gentlemen, he said,
And share my bed with Capricorn and Cancer.

II

Death is all metaphors, shape in one history;
The child that sucketh long is shooting up,
The planet-ducted pelican of circles
Weans on an artery the genders strip;
Child of the short spark in a shapeless country
Soon sets alight a long stick from the cradle;
The horizontal cross-bones of Abaddon,
You by the cavern over the black stairs,
Rung bone and blade, the verticals of Adam,
And, manned by midnight, Jacob to the stars.
Hairs of your head, then said the hollow agent,
Are but the roots of nettles and feathers
Over the groundworks thrusting through a pavement
And hemlock-headed in the wood of weathers.

III

First there was the lamb on knocking knees
And three dead seasons on a climbing grave
That Adam's wether in the flock of horns,
Butt of the tree-tailed worm that mounted Eve,
Horned down with skullfoot and the skull of toes
On thunderous pavements in the garden of time;
Rip of the vaults, I took my marrow-ladle
Out of the wrinkled undertaker's van,
And, Rip Van Winkle from a timeless cradle,
Dipped me breast-deep in the descending bone;
The black ram, shuffling of the year, old winter,
Alone alive among his mutton fold,
We rung our weathering changes on the ladder,
Said the antipodes, and twice spring chimed.

IV

What is the metre of the dictionary?
The size of genesis? the short spark's gender?
Shade without shape? the shape of the Pharaohs echo?
(My shape of age nagging the wounded whisper.)
Which sixth of wind blew out the burning gentry?
(Questions are hunchbacks to the poker marrow.)
What of a bamboo man amomg your acres?
Corset the boneyards for a crooked boy?
Button your bodice on a hump of splinters,
My camel's eyes will needle through the shroud.
Loves reflection of the mushroom features,
Still snapped by night in the bread-sided field,
Once close-up smiling in the wall of pictures,
Arc-lamped thrown back upon the cutting flood.

V

And from the windy West came two-gunned Gabriel,
From Jesu's sleeve trumped up the king of spots,
The sheath-decked jacks, queen with a shuffled heart;
Said the fake gentleman in suit of spades,
Black-tongued and tipsy from salvation's bottle.
Rose my Byzantine Adam in the night.
For loss of blood I fell on Ishmael's plain,
Under the milky mushrooms slew my hunger,
A climbing sea from Asia had me down
And Jonah's Moby snatched me by the hair,
Cross-stroked salt Adam to the frozen angel
Pin-legged on pole-hills with a black medusa
By waste seas where the white bear quoted Virgil
And sirens singing from our lady's sea-straw.

VI

Cartoon of slashes on the tide-traced crater,

He in a book of water tallow-eyed

By lava's light split through the oyster vowels

And burned sea silence on a wick of words.

Pluck, cock, my sea eye, said medusa's scripture,

Lop, love, my fork tongue, said the pin-hilled nettle;

And love plucked out the stinging siren's eye,

Old cock from nowheres lopped the minstrel tongue

Till tallow I blew from the wax's tower

The fats of midnight when the salt was singing;

Adam, time's joker, on a witch of cardboard

Spelt out the seven seas, an evil index,

The bagpipe-breasted ladies in the deadweed

Blew out the blood gauze through the wound of manwax.

VII

Now stamp the Lord's Prayer on a grain of rice,
A Bible-leaved of all the written woods
Strip to this tree: a rocking alphabet,
Genesis in the root, the scarecrow word,
And one light's language in the book of trees.
Doom on deniers at the wind-turned statement.
Time's tune my ladies with the teats of music,
The scaled sea-sawers, fix in a naked sponge
Who sucks the bell-voiced Adam out of magic,
Time, milk, and magic, from the world beginning.
Time is the tune my ladies lend their heartbreak,
From bald pavilions and the house of bread
Time tracks the sound of shape on man and cloud,
On rose and icicle the ringing handprint.

VIII

This was the crucifixion on the mountain,
Time's nerve in vinegar, the gallow grave
As tarred with blood as the bright thorns I wept;
The world's my wound, God's Mary in her grief,
Bent like three trees and bird-papped through her shift,
With pins for teardrops is the long wound's woman.
This was the sky, Jack Christ, each minstrel angle
Drove in the heaven-driven of the nails
Till the three-coloured rainbow from my nipples
From pole to pole leapt round the snail-waked world.
I by the tree of thieves, all glory's sawbones,
Unsex the skeleton this mountain minute,
And by this blowcock witness of the sun
Suffer the heaven's children through my heartbeat.

IX

From the oracular archives and the parchment,
Prophets and fibre kings in oil and letter,
The lamped calligrapher, the queen in splints,
Buckle to lint and cloth their natron footsteps,
Draw on the glove of prints, dead Cairo's henna
Pour like a halo on the caps and serpents.
This was the resurrection in the desert,
Death from a bandage, rants the mask of scholars
Gold on such features, and the linen spirit
Weds my long gentleman to dusts and furies;
With priest and pharaoh bed my gentle wound,
World in the sand, on the triangle landscape,
With stones of odyssey for ash and garland
And rivers of the dead around my neck.

X

Let the tale's sailor from a Christian voyage
Atlaswise hold half-way off the dummy bay
Time's ship-racked gospel on the globe I balance:
So shall winged harbours through the rockbird's eyes
Spot the blown word, and on the seas I image
December's thorn screwed in a brow of holly.
Let the first Peter from a rainbow's quayrail
Ask the tall fish swept from the bible east,
What rhubarb man peeled in her foam-blue channel
Has sown a flying garden round that sea-ghost?
Green as beginning, let the garden diving
Soar, with its two bark towers, to that Day
When the worm builds with the gold straws of venom
My nest of mercies in the rude, red tree.

A Grief Ago

A grief ago,
She who was who I hold, the fats and the flower,
Or, water-lammed, from the scythe-sided thorn,
Hell wind and sea,
A stem cementing, wrestled up the tower,
Rose maid and male,
Or, master venus, through the paddler's bowl
Sailed up the sun;

Who is my grief,
A chrysalis unwrinkling on the iron,
Wrenched by my fingerman, the leaden bud
Shot through the leaf,
Was who was folded on the rod the aaron
Road east to plague,
The horn and ball of water on the frog
Housed in the side.

And she who lies,
Like exodus a chapter from the garden,
Brand of the lily's anger on her ring,
Tugged through the days
Her ropes of heritage, the wars of pardon,
On field and sand
The twelve triangles of the cherub wind
Engraving going.

Who then is she,
She holding me? The people's sea drives on her,
Drives out the father from the caesared camp;
The dens of shape
Shape all her whelps with the long voice of water,
That she I have,
The country-handed grave boxed into love,
Rise before dark.

The night is near,
A nitric shape that leaps her, time and acid;
I tell her this: before the suncock cast
Her bone to fire,
Let her inhale her dead, through seed and solid
Draw in their seas,
So cross her hand with their grave gipsy eyes,
And close her fist.

I Make this in a Warring Absence

I make this in a warring absence when
Each ancient, stone-necked minute of love's season
Harbours my anchored tongue, slips the quaystone,
When, praise is blessed, her pride in mast and fountain
Sailed and set dazzling by the handshaped ocean,
In that proud sailing tree with branches driven
Through the last vault and vegetable groyne,
And this weak house to marrow-columned heaven,

Is corner-cast, breath's rag, scrawled weed, a vain
And opium head, crow stalk, puffed, cut, and blown,
Or like the tide-looped breastknot reefed again
Or rent ancestrally the roped sea-hymen,
And, pride is last, is like a child alone
By magnet winds to her blind mother drawn,
Bread and milk mansion in a toothless town.

She makes for me a nettle's innocence
And a silk pigeon's guilt in her proud absence,
In the molested rocks the shell of virgins,
The frank, closed pearl, the sea-girls' lineaments
Glint in the staved and siren-printed caverns,
Is maiden in the shameful oak, omens
Whalebed and bulldance, the gold bush of lions,
Proud as a sucked stone and huge as sandgrains.

These are her contraries: the beast who follows
With priest's grave foot and hand of five assassins
Her molten flight up cinder-nesting columns,
Calls the starved fire herd, is cast in ice,
Lost in a limp-treed and uneating silence,
Who scales a hailing hill in her cold flintsteps
Falls on a ring of summers and locked noons.

I make a weapon of an ass's skeleton
And walk the warring sands by the dead town.
Cudgel great air, wreck east, and topple sundown,
Storm her sped heart, hang with beheaded veins
Its wringing shell, and let her eyelids fasten.
Destruction, picked by birds, brays through the jaw-bone,

And, for that murder's sake, dark with contagion
Like an approaching wave I sprawl to ruin.
Ruin, the room of errors, one rood dropped
Down the stacked sea and water-pillared shade,
Weighed in rock shroud, is my proud pyramid;
Where, wound in emerald linen and sharp wind,
The hero's head lies scraped of every legend,
Comes love's anatomist with sun-gloved hand
Who picks the live heart on a diamond.

'His mother's womb had a tongue that lapped up mud,'
Cried the topless, inchtaped lips from hank and hood
In that bright anchorground where I lay linened,
'A lizard darting with black venom's thread
Doubled, to fork him back, through the lockjaw bed
And the breath-white, curtained mouth of seed.'
'See,' drummed the taut masks, 'how the dead ascend:
In the groin's endless coil a man is tangled.'

These once-blind eyes have breathed a wind of visions,
The cauldron's root through this once-rindless hand
Fumed like a tree, and tossed a burning bird;
With loud, torn tooth and tail and cobweb drum
The crumpled packs fled past this ghost in bloom,
And, mild as pardon from a cloud of pride,
The terrible world my brother bares his skin.

Now in the cloud's big breast lie quiet countries,
Delivered seas my love from her proud place
Walks with no wound, nor lightning in her face,
A calm wind blows that raised the trees like hair
Once where the soft snow's blood was turned to ice.
And though my love pulls the pale, nippled air,
Prides of to-morrow suckling in her eyes,
Yet this I make in a forgiving presence.

When All My Five and Country Senses See

When all my five and country senses see,
The fingers will forget green thumbs and mark
How, through the halfmoon's vegetable eye,
Husk of young stars and handfull zodiac,
Love in the frost is pared and wintered by,
The whispering ears will watch love drummed away
Down breeze and shell to a discordant beach,
And, lashed to syllables, the lynx tongue cry
That her fond wounds are mended bitterly.
My nostrils see her breath burn like a bush.

My one and noble heart has witnesses
In all love's countries, that will grope awake;
And when blind sleep drops on the spying senses,
The heart is sensual, though five eyes break.

Paper and Sticks

Paper and sticks and shovel and match
Why won't the news of the old world catch
And the fire in a temper start

Once I had a rich boy for myself
I loved his body and his navy blue wealth
And I lived in his purse and his heart

When in our bed I was tossing and turning
All I could see were his brown eyes burning
By the green of a one pound note

I talk to him as I clean the grate
O my dear it's never too late
To take me away as you whispered and wrote

I had a handsome and well-off boy
I'll share my money and we'll run for joy
With a bouncing and silver spooned kid

On a Wedding Anniversary

The sky is torn across
This ragged anniversary of two
Who moved for three years in tune
Down the long walks of their vows.

Now their love lies a loss
And Love and his patients roar on a chain;
From every tune or crater
Carrying cloud, Death strikes their house.

Too late in the wrong rain
They come together whom their love parted:
The windows pour into their heart
And the doors burn in their brain.

Love in the Asylum

        A stranger has come
To share my room in the house not right in the head,
        A girl mad as birds

Bolting the night of the door with her arm her plume.
        Strait in the mazed bed
She deludes the heaven-proof house with entering clouds

Yet she deludes with walking the nightmarish room,
        At large as the dead,
Or rides the imagined oceans of the male wards.

        She has come possessed
Who admits the delusive light through the bouncing wall,
        Possessed by the skies

She sleeps in the narrow trough yet she walks the dust
        Yet raves at her will
On the madhouse boards worn thin by my walking tears.

And taken by light in her arms at long and dear last
                I may without fail
Suffer the first vision that set fire to the stars.

The Ballad of the Long-Legged Bait

The bows glided down, and the coast
Blackened with birds took a last look
At his thrashing hair and whale-blue eye;
The trodden town rang its cobbles for luck.

Then good-bye to the fishermanned
Boat with its anchor free and fast
As a bird hooking over the sea,
High and dry by the top of the mast,

Whispered the affectionate sand
And the bulwarks of the dazzled quay.
For my sake sail, and never look back,
Said the looking land.

Sails drank the wind, and white as milk
He sped into the drinking dark;
The sun shipwrecked west on a pearl
And the moon swam out of its hulk.

Funnels and masts went by in a whirl.
Good-bye to the man on the sea-legged deck
To the gold gut that sings on his reel
To the bait that stalked out of the sack,

For we saw him throw to the swift flood
A girl alive with his hooks through her lips;
All the fishes were rayed in blood,
Said the dwindling ships.

Good-bye to chimneys and funnels,
Old wives that spin in the smoke,
He was blind to the eyes of candles
In the praying windows of waves

But heard his bait buck in the wake
And tussle in a shoal of loves.
Now cast down your rod, for the whole
Of the sea is hilly with whales,

She longs among horses and angels,
The rainbow-fish bend in her joys,
Floated the lost cathedral
Chimes of the rocked buoys.

Where the anchor rode like a gull
Miles over the moonstruck boat
A squall of birds bellowed and fell,
A cloud blew the rain from its throat;

He saw the storm smoke out to kill
With fuming bows and ram of ice,
Fire on starlight, rake Jesu's stream;
And nothing shone on the water's face

But the oil and bubble of the moon,
Plunging and piercing in his course
The lured fish under the foam
Witnessed with a kiss.

Whales in the wake like capes and Alps
Quaked the sick sea and snouted deep,
Deep the great bushed bait with raining lips
Slipped the fins of those humpbacked tons

And fled their love in a weaving dip.
Oh, Jericho was falling in their lungs!
She nipped and dived in the nick of love,
Spun on a spout like a long-legged ball

Till every beast blared down in a swerve
Till every turtle crushed from his shell
Till every bone in the rushing grave
Rose and crowed and fell!

Good luck to the hand on the rod,
There is thunder under its thumbs;
Gold gut is a lightning thread,
His fiery reel sings off its flames,

The whirled boat in the burn of his blood
Is crying from nets to knives,
Oh the shearwater birds and their boatsized brood
Oh the bulls of Biscay and their calves

Are making under the green, laid veil
The long-legged beautiful bait their wives.
Break the black news and paint on a sail
Huge weddings in the waves,

Over the wakeward-flashing spray
Over the gardens of the floor
Clash out the mounting dolphin's day,
My mast is a bell-spire,

Strike and smoothe, for my decks are drums,
Sing through the water-spoken prow
The octopus walking into her limbs
The polar eagle with his tread of snow.

From salt-lipped beak to the kick of the stern
Sing how the seal has kissed her dead!
The long, laid minute's bride drifts on
Old in her cruel bed.

Over the graveyard in the water
Mountains and galleries beneath
Nightingale and hyena
Rejoicing for that drifting death

Sing and howl through sand and anemone
Valley and sahara in a shell,
Oh all the wanting flesh his enemy
Thrown to the sea in the shell of a girl

Is old as water and plain as an eel;
Always good-bye to the long-legged bread
Scattered in the paths of his heels
For the salty birds fluttered and fed

And the tall grains foamed in their bills;
Always good-bye to the fires of the face,
For the crab-backed dead on the sea-bed rose
And scuttled over her eyes,

The blind, clawed stare is cold as sleet.
The tempter under the eyelid
Who shows to the selves asleep
Mast-high moon-white women naked

Walking in wishes and lovely for shame
Is dumb and gone with his flame of brides.
Susannah's drowned in the bearded stream
And no-one stirs at Sheba's side

But the hungry kings of the tides;
Sin who had a woman's shape
Sleeps till Silence blows on a cloud
And all the lifted waters walk and leap.

Lucifer that bird's dropping
Out of the sides of the north
Has melted away and is lost
Is always lost in her vaulted breath,

Venus lies star-struck in her wound
And the sensual ruins make
Seasons over the liquid world,
White springs in the dark.

Always good-bye, cried the voices through the shell,
Good-bye always, for the flesh is cast
And the fisherman winds his reel
With no more desire than a ghost.

Always good luck, praised the finned in the feather
Bird after dark and the laughing fish
As the sails drank up the hail of thunder
And the long-tailed lightning lit his catch.

The boat swims into the six-year weather,
A wind throws a shadow and it freezes fast.
See what the gold gut drags from under
Mountains and galleries to the crest!

See what clings to hair and skull
As the boat skims on with drinking wings!
The statues of great rain stand still,
And the flakes fall like hills.

Sing and strike his heavy haul
Toppling up the boatside in a snow of light!
His decks are drenched with miracles.
Oh miracle of fishes! The long dead bite!

Out of the urn a size of a man
Out of the room the weight of his trouble
Out of the house that holds a town
In the continent of a fossil

One by one in dust and shawl,
Dry as echoes and insect-faced,
His fathers cling to the hand of the girl
And the dead hand leads the past,

Leads them as children and as air
On to the blindly tossing tops;
The centuries throw back their hair
And the old men sing from newborn lips:

Time is bearing another son.
Kill Time! She turns in her pain!
The oak is felled in the acorn
And the hawk in the egg kills the wren.

He who blew the great fire in
And died on a hiss of flames
Or walked the earth in the evening
Counting the denials of the grains

Clings to her drifting hair, and climbs;
And he who taught their lips to sing
Weeps like the risen sun among
The liquid choirs of his tribes.

The rod bends low, divining land,
And through the sundered water crawls
A garden holding to her hand
With birds and animals

With men and women and waterfalls
Trees cool and dry in the whirlpool of ships
And stunned and still on the green, laid veil
Sand with legends in its virgin laps

And prophets loud on the burned dunes;
Insects and valleys hold her thighs hard,
Times and places grip her breast bone,
She is breaking with seasons and clouds;

Round her trailed wrist fresh water weaves,
with moving fish and rounded stones
Up and down the greater waves
A separate river breathes and runs;

Strike and sing his catch of fields
For the surge is sown with barley,
The cattle graze on the covered foam,
The hills have footed the waves away,

With wild sea fillies and soaking bridles
With salty colts and gales in their limbs
All the horses of his haul of miracles
Gallop through the arched, green farms,

Trot and gallop with gulls upon them
And thunderbolts in their manes.
O Rome and Sodom To-morrow and London
The country tide is cobbled with towns

And steeples pierce the cloud on her shoulder
And the streets that the fisherman combed
When his long-legged flesh was a wind on fire
And his loin was a hunting flame

Coil from the thoroughfares of her hair
And terribly lead him home alive
Lead her prodigal home to his terror,
The furious ox-killing house of love.

Down, down, down, under the ground,
Under the floating villages,
Turns the moon-chained and water-wound
Metropolis of fishes,

There is nothing left of the sea but its sound,
Under the earth the loud sea walks,
In deathbeds of orchards the boat dies down
And the bait is drowned among hayricks,

Land, land, land, nothing remains
Of the pacing, famous sea but its speech,
And into its talkative seven tombs
The anchor dives through the floors of a church.

Good-bye, good luck, struck the sun and the moon,
To the fisherman lost on the land.
He stands alone in the door of his home,
With his long-legged heart in his hand.

Into Her Lying Down Head

I

Into her lying down head
His enemies entered bed,
Under the encumbered eyelid,
Through the rippled drum of the hair-buried ear;
And Noah's rekindled now unkind dove
Flew man-bearing there.
Last night in a raping wave
Whales unreined from the green grave
In fountains of origin gave up their love,
Along her innocence glided
Jaun aflame and savagely young King Lear,
Queen Catherine howling bare
And Samson drowned in his hair,
The colossal intimacies of silent
Once seen strangers or shades on a stair;
There the dark blade and wanton sighing her down
To a haycock couch and the scythes of his arms
Rode and whistled a hundred times
Before the crowing morning climbed;
Man was the burning England she was sleep-walking, and the enamouring island

    Made her limbs blind by luminous charms,
Sleep to a newborn sleep in a swaddling loin-leaf stroked and sang
    And his runaway beloved childlike laid in the acorned sand.

II

There where a numberless tongue
        Wound their room with a male moan,
    His faith around her flew undone
And darkness hung the walls with baskets of snakes,
A furnace-nostrilled column-membered
            Super-or-near man
        Resembling to her dulled sense
        The thief of adolescence,
Early imaginary half remembered
        Oceanic lover alone
Jealousy cannot forget for all her sakes,
        Made his bad bed in her good
        Night, and enjoyed as he would.
Crying, white gowned, from the middle moonlit stages
        Out to the tiered and hearing tide,
Close and far she announced the theft of the heart
In the taken body at many ages,
        Trespasser and broken bride
        Celebrating at her side
All blood-signed assailing and vanished marriages in which he had no lovely part

      Nor could share, for his pride, to the least
Mutter and foul wingbeat of the solemnizing nightpriest
Her holy unholy hours with the always anonymous beast.

III

        Two sand grains together in bed,
        Head to heaven-circling head,
    Singly lie with the whole wide shore,
The covering sea their nightfall with no names;
And out of every domed and soil-based shell
        One voice in chains declaims
      The female, deadly, and male
      Libidinous betrayal,
Golden dissolving under the water veil.
    A she bird sleeping brittle by
Her lover's wings that fold to-morrow's flight,
        Within the nested treefork
        Sings to the treading hawk
Carrion, paradise, chirrup my bright yolk.
    A blade of grass longs with the meadow,
A stone lies lost and locked in the lark-high hill.
Open as to the air to the naked shadow
        O she lies alone and still,
        Innocent between two wars,
With the incestuous secret brother in the seconds to perpetuate the stars,
    A man torn up mourns in the sole night.

And the second comers, the severers, the enemies from the deep
Forgotten dark, rest their pulse and bury their dead in her
   faithless sleep.

Lie Still, Sleep Becalmed

Lie still, sleep becalmed, sufferer with the wound
In the throat, burning and turning. All night afloat
On the silent sea we have heard the sound
That came from the wound wrapped in the salt sheet.

Under the mile off moon we trembled listening
To the sea sound flowing like blood from the loud wound
And when the salt sheet broke in a storm of singing
The voices of all the drowned swam on the wind.

Open a pathway through the slow sad sail,
Throw wide to the wind the gates of the wandering boat
For my voyage to begin to the end of my wound,
We heard the sea sound sing, we saw the salt sheet tell.
Lie still, sleep becalmed, hide the mouth in the throat,
Or we shall obey, and ride with you through the drowned.

In My Craft or Sullen Art

In my craft or sullen art
Exercised in the still night
When only the moon rages
And the lovers lie abed
With all their griefs in their arms,
I labour by singing light
Not for ambition or bread
Or the strut and trade of charms
On the ivory stages
But for the common wages
Of their most secret heart.

Not for the proud man apart
From the raging moon I write
On these spindrift pages
Nor for the towering dead
With their nightingales and psalms
But for the lovers, their arms
Round the griefs of the ages,
Who pay no praise or wages
Nor heed my craft or art.

The Conversation of Prayers

The conversation of prayers about to be said
By the child going to bed and the man on the stairs
Who climbs to his dying love in her high room,
The one not caring to whom in his sleep he will move
And the other full of tears that she will be dead,

Turns in the dark on the sound they know will arise
Into the answering skies from the green ground,
From the man on the stairs and the child by his bed.
The sound about to be said in the two prayers
For the sleep in a safe land and the love who dies

Will be the same grief flying. Whom shall they calm?
Shall the child sleep unharmed or the man be crying?
The conversation of prayers about to be said
Turns on the quick and the dead, and the man on the stairs
To-night shall find no dying but alive and warm

In the fire of his care his love in the high room.
And the child not caring to whom he climbs his prayer
Shall drown in a grief as deep as his true grave,
And mark the dark eyed wave, through the eyes of sleep,
Dragging him up the stairs to one who lies dead.

In the White Giant's Thigh

Through throats where many rivers meet, the curlews cry
Under the conceiving moon, on the high chalk hill,
And there this night I walk in the white giant's thigh
Where barren as boulders women lie longing still

To labour and love though they lay down long ago.

Through throats where many rivers meet, the women pray,
Pleading in the waded bay for the seed to flow
Though the names on their weed grown stones are rained away

And alone in the night's eternal, curving act
They yearn with tongues of curlews for the unconceived
And immemorial sons of the cudgelling, hacked

Hill. Who once in gooseskin winter loved all ice leaved
In the courters' lanes, or twined in the ox roasting sun
In the wains tonned so high that the wisps of the hay
Clung to the pitching clouds, or gay with any one
Young as they in the after milking moonlight lay

Under the lighted shapes of faith and their moonshade
Petticoats galed high, or shy with the rough riding boys,
Now clasp me to their grains in the gigantic glade,

Who once, green countries since, were a hedgerow of joys.

Time by, their dust was flesh the swineherd rooted sly,
Flared in the reek of the wiving sty with the rush
Light of his thighs, spreadeagle to the dunghill sky,
Or with their orchard man in the core of the sun's bush
Rough as cows' tongues and trashed with brambles their buttermilk
Manes, under his quenchless summer barbed gold to the bone,

Or rippling soft in the spinney moon as the silk
And ducked and draked white lake that harps to a hail stone.

Who once were a bloom of wayside brides in the hawed house
And heard the lewd, wooed field flow to the coming frost,
The scurrying, furred small friars squeal, in the dowse
Of day, in the thistle aisles, till the white owl crossed

Their breast, the vaulting does roister, the horned bucks climb
Quick in the wood at love, where a torch of foxes foams,
All birds and beasts of the linked night uproar and chime

And the mole snout blunt under his pilgrimage of domes,
Or, butter fat goosegirls, bounced in a gambo bed,
Their breasts full of honey, under their gander king
Trounced by his wings in the hissing shippen, long dead
And gone that barley dark where their clogs danced in the spring,
And their firefly hairpins flew, and the ricks ran round—
(But nothing bore, no mouthing babe to the veined hives
Hugged, and barren and bare on Mother Goose's ground
They with the simple Jacks were a boulder of wives)—

Now curlew cry me down to kiss the mouths of their dust.

The dust of their kettles and clocks swings to and fro
Where the hay rides now or the bracken kitchens rust
As the arc of the billhooks that flashed the hedges low
And cut the birds' boughs that the minstrel sap ran red.
They from houses where the harvest bows, hold me hard,
Who heard the tall bell sail down the Sundays of the dead
And the rain wring out its tongues on the faded yard,
Teach me the love that is evergreen after the fall leaved

Grave, after Beloved on the grass gulfed cross is scrubbed
Off by the sun and Daughters no longer grieved
Save by their long desirers in the fox cubbed
Streets or hungering in the crumbled wood: to these
Hale dead and deathless do the women of the hill
Love for ever meridian through the courters' trees

And the daughters of darkness flame like Fawkes fires still.

Lament

When I was a windy boy and a bit
And the black spit of the chapel fold,
(Sighed the old ram rod, dying of women),
I tiptoed shy in the gooseberry wood,
The rude owl cried like a tell-tale tit,
I skipped in a blush as the big girls rolled
Nine-pin down on donkey's common,
And on seesaw sunday nights I wooed
Whoever I would with my wicked eyes,
The whole of the moon I could love and leave
All the green leaved little weddings' wives
In the coal black bush and let them grieve.

When I was a gusty man and a half
And the black beast of the beetles' pews
(Sighed the old ram rod, dying of bitches),
Not a boy and a bit in the wick–
Dipping moon and drunk as a new dropped calf,
I whistled all night in the twisted flues,
Midwives grew in the midnight ditches,
And the sizzling sheets of the town cried, Quick!—

Whenever I dove in a breast high shoal,
Wherever I ramped in the clover quilts,
Whatsoever I did in the coal-
Black night, I left my quivering prints.

When I was a man you could call a man
And the black cross of the holy house,
(Sighed the old ram rod, dying of welcome),
Brandy and ripe in my bright, bass prime,
No springtailed tom in the red hot town
With every simmering woman his mouse
But a hillocky bull in the swelter
Of summer come in his great good time
To the sultry, biding herds, I said,
Oh, time enough when the blood runs cold,
And I lie down but to sleep in bed,
For my sulking, skulking, coal black soul!

When I was half the man I was
And serve me right as the preachers warn,
(Sighed the old ram rod, dying of downfall),
No flailing calf or cat in a flame
Or hickory bull in milky grass

But a black sheep with a crumpled horn,
At last the soul from its foul mousehole
Slunk pouting out when the limp time came;
And I gave my soul a blind, slashed eye,
Gristle and rind, and a roarers' life,
And I shoved it into the coal black sky
To find a woman's soul for a wife.

Now I am a man no more no more
And a black reward for a roaring life,
(Sighed the old ram rod, dying of strangers),
Tidy and cursed in my dove cooed room
I lie down thin and hear the good bells jaw—
For, oh, my soul found a sunday wife
In the coal black sky and she bore angels!
Harpies around me out of her womb!
Chastity prays for me, piety sings,
Innocence sweetens my last black breath,
Modesty hides my thighs in her wings,
And all the deadly virtues plague my death!

Bibliography

'Especially when the October Wind'. Written in 1932. First published in the *Listener*, October 1934. Published in *18 Poems*, 1934.

'The Hunchback in the Park'. Written in May 1932. First published in *Life and Letters Today*, October 1941. Published in *New Poems*, 1943.

'I Have Longed to Move Away'. Written in March 1933. First published in the *New Verse*, December 1935. Published in *25 Poems*, 1936.

'Find Meat on Bones'. Written July 1933. First published in *Purpose*, April-June 1936. Published in *25 Poems,* 1934.

'The Tombstone Told When She Died'. Written in July 1933. First published in *Seven*, Winter 1938. Published in *The Map of Love*, 1939.

'In the Beginning'. Written in September 1933. First published in *18 Poems*, 1934. Published in *18 Poems*, 1934.

'From Love's First Fever to Her Plague'. Written in October 1933. First published in the *Criterion*, October 1934. Published in *18 Poems*, 1934.

'When Once the Twilight Locks No Longer'. Written in November 1933. First published in the *New Verse*, June 1934. Published in *18 Poems*, 1934.

'Should Lanterns Shine'. Written in 1934. First published in *New Verse*, December 1935. Published in *25 Poems,* 1934.

'Where Once the Waters of Your Face'. Written in March 1934. First published in *Sunday Referee*, March 1934. Published in *18 Poems*, 1934.

'If I Were Tickled by the Rub of Love'. Written in April 1934. First published in the *New Verse*, August 1934. Published in *18 Poems*, 1934.

'Altarwise by Owl-Light'. Written in December 1934. First published in *Life and Letters Today*, December 1935. Published in *25 Poems,* 1934.

'A Grief Ago'. Written in January 1935. First published in *Programme,* October 1935. Published in *25 Poems,* 1934.

'I Make this in a Warring Absence'. Written in 1937. First published in *Twentieth Century Verse*, January-February 1938. Published in *The Map of Love*, 1939.

'When All My Five and Country Senses See'. First published in *Poetry* (Chicago), August 1938. Published in *The Map of Love*, 1939.

'Paper and Sticks'. Written in 1939. First published in *Seven*, Autumn 1939. Published in *Deaths and Entrances*, 1946.

'On a Wedding Anniversary'. Written in July 1940. First published in *Poetry* (London), January 1941. Published in *The Map of Love*, 1939.

'Love in the Asylum'. Written in 1941. First published in *Poetry* (London), May-June 1941. Published in *New Poems,* 1943.

'The Ballad of the Long-Legged Bait'. First published in *Horizon*, July 1941. Published in *New Poems*, 1943.

'Into Her Lying Down Head'. Written in 1940. First published in *Life and Letters Today*, November 1940. Published in *New Poems*, 1943.

'Lie Still, Sleep Becalmed'. Written in 1944. First published in *Life and Letters Today*, June 1945. Published in *Deaths and Entrances*, 1946.

'In My Craft or Sullen Art'. Written in 1945. First published in *Life and Letters Today*, October 1945. Published in *Deaths and Entrances*, 1946.

'The Conversation of Prayers'. Written in March 1945. First published in the *New Republic*, July 1945. Published in *Deaths and Entrances*, 1946.

'In the White Giant's Thigh'. First published in *Botteghe Oscure* (Rome), November 1950. Published in *In Country Sleep*, 1952

'Lament'. First published in *Botteghe Oscure* (Rome), November 1951. Published *In Country Sleep*, 1952

More from Ragged Hand

Rage Against the Dying of the Light
Collected Poems of Death, Loss, & Grief
By Dylan Thomas
ISBN: 9781528723411
A richly powerful collection of poetry traversing the inevitability of death as Dylan Thomas explores the complicated themes of grief and loss.

To the Trees and the Stones
Collected Poems of Nature
By Dylan Thomas
ISBN: 9781528723404
This pocket-sized collection of ethereal nature poetry from Dylan Thomas unveils his deep appreciation for the beauty of nature and the natural world.

In My Craft or Sullen Art
The Selected Poetry of Dylan Thomas
ISBN: 9781528723381
A hauntingly beautiful introduction to one of the greatest literary voices in Welsh history, this collection celebrates the intensely emotional and lyrical poetry of Dylan Thomas.

How to be a Poet
The Collected Short Stories & Essays of Dylan Thomas
ISBN: 9781528723428
Discover the witty memoirs, stirring prose, and insightful essays of one of the greatest Welsh writers in literary history.

Portrait of the Artist as a Young Dog
By Dylan Thomas
ISBN: 9781528723442
Delve into the mind and life of the prolific Welsh poet Dylan Thomas in this roguish collection of short autobiographical stories.

A Child's Christmas in Wales
Illustrated Edition
By Dylan Thomas
ISBN: 9781528723435
Capturing the nostalgia of timeless tradition, childhood wonder, and festive magic, Dylan Thomas reminisces in this magically illustrated tale of Christmas in the heart of the Welsh countryside.